A Pil
With The Angels

A Journal for Prayer and
Reflection to Grow in Virtue

rekindle. renew. reCatholic.

Rediscover the Adventure of Faith

God regularly gives unique moments of grace and calls us to Himself. That is an invitation for the Church to continually rediscover the hidden treasure of our Catholic faith, rekindle a passionate love for it, and allow it to renew our lives.

reCatholic is a response to God's personal call for us by creating resources for groups and individuals that inspire and challenge Catholics to rediscover, rekindle, and renew their faith so it becomes a life-changing adventure and the greatest source of fulfillment.

For more information visit reCatholic.org

Holy Angels Academy

Our Mission

Our mission is to educate and form our youth by the means of Catholic schooling in the classical tradition, so as to prepare them to lead holy and honorable lives for God and country and thus attain the end for which they were created, that is, eternal happiness with God.

Our Beginning

In the early 1970s, a small group of lay faithful sought the help of a Dominican Sister to establish a school to provide authentic Catholic education for our young people. At a time when many teachings of the Faith were being called into question and secular influences were impacting public as well as Catholic education at all levels, there were those, lay and religious, who acted to establish private schools that would preserve Catholic education in accord with the Magisterium of the Church, profess a special fidelity to the Holy Father, and a love and respect for the local Bishop.

Our Founder

Sister Mary Elise Groves, O.P., a native of Louisville, was a promoter and defender of truth, always faithful to the Dominican motto, *Veritas*. With many years of experience as an administrator and teacher at the elementary and secondary levels, Sister Elise would use her fine Dominican training to lay a foundation for what Holy Angels is today.

A Pilgrim's Prayer

Adapted from an ancient prayer that concludes the Camino de Santiago Pilgrims' Mass.

O God, who brought Your servant Abraham out of the land of the Chaldeans, protecting him in his wandering across the desert, we ask that You watch over us, Your servants, as we walk in the love of Your name toward our heavenly home.

Be for us our companion on the walk,

Our guide at the crossroads,

Our breath in our weariness,

Our protection in danger,

Our home on the path,

Our shade in the heat,

Our light in the darkness,

Our consolation in our discouragements,

And our strength in our intentions.

So that with Your guidance we may arrive safe and sound at the end of the road enriched with grace and virtue and filled with joy as we behold You face to face. In the name of Jesus Christ our Lord, Amen.

St. James, pray for us.

Our Lady of Fatima, pray for us.

Table of Contents

Introduction   9
How to Use this Prayer Journal   13
Origin   **15**
  Faith   17
  Humility   21
  Religion   25
  Interior Silence   29
  Simplicity   33
  Gratitude   37
Fiat   **45**
  Hope   47
  Obedience   51
  Meekness   55
  Generosity   59
  Patience   63
  Prudence   67
Sacrifice   **75**
  Love   77
  Fortitude   81
  Temperance   85
  Justice   89
  Chastity   93
  Diligence   97
Transfiguration   **105**
  Charity   107
  Truthfulness   111
  Kindness   115
  Forgiveness   119
  Constancy   123
  Perseverance   127

Introduction

An Everyday Pilgrimage

According to Pope Benedict XVI in his visit to Compostela on November 6, 2010: "To go on pilgrimage really means to step out of ourselves in order to encounter God where he has revealed himself, where his grace has shone with particular splendor and produced rich fruits of conversion and holiness among those who believe."

This prayer journal is meant to be an everyday pilgrimage, where we can encounter God firstly in Scripture, but also in our daily lives. Daily reflections help us ponder God's action in us and how we can respond to His love.

The pontiff continues: "May the joy of knowing that you are God's beloved children bring you to an ever deeper love for the Church and to cooperate with her in her work of leading all men and women to Christ."

The Stages of Pilgrimage

I. Origin
Our pilgrimage on earth begins with the foundation of faith and gratitude. God is the origin of our journey and is the first to call us to Himself.

II. Fiat
Just like the Blessed Virgin Mary, our lives require a response, a "fiat" to God's invitation. This requires trust and obedience.

III. Sacrifice
Our response leads to true love and fortitude as we give of ourselves to God and to our brothers and sisters in Christ and take on the responsibilities of justice.

IV. Transfiguration
Like the examples we find in the saints, we too are called to be transformed into Christ and to persevere in His name.

Twenty Four Virtues

For each stage of pilgrimage there are six virtues that summarize a part of our spiritual journey. This journal can be used as a personal guide to prayer or can accompany families in their established prayer routines.

The purpose of this journal is to give you a way to systematically make an everyday Pilgrimage during your time of prayer.

You may reflect on one virtue per day, for example, or one per week, as best suits your personal needs. You may choose to reflect on the virtues in the order given or choose to select the particular virtue that speaks to your heart at the moment. There is no right or wrong way to use this prayer journal.

A Summary of the Spiritual Life

Our pilgrimage on earth can be summarized by our growth in virtue. This prayer journal systematically covers the most common Catholic virtues and makes it easy for individuals and families to pray about them and to reflect on concrete ways to grow.

How to Use this Prayer Journal

Reflect and Pray with Each Virtue

Scripture Passage
Brief passages from the Bible can help you learn about each virtue. There are a variety of passages, from the Old and New Testaments. God's word is living and active and He continues to speak to you today through Sacred Scripture.

Virtue Prayer
Each virtue prayer can accompany you during the day or the week as a gentle reminder to ask for God's help. If the journal is used as a family, this prayer could also be added to family prayer time or to your prayers before meals.

Personal Reflection
Questions have been provided to help you reflect on the Scripture passages. Quiet your heart to listen to God's voice, then thank Him for His guidance, finally, look for concrete ways to apply His grace concretely to your life.

Space for Journaling
Journaling is recommended for jotting down spiritual insights that you have gathered, people or intentions you would like to pray for, things you are grateful for, and any resolutions you would like to remember from your time of prayer.

Origin

The Foundation of Faith

Our pilgrimage on earth begins with the foundation of faith and gratitude. God is the origin of our journey and is the first to call us to Himself.

The Meaning of this Glyph

The sun symbolizes the beginning of a journey. The Church building represents our initial encounter with God, which often takes place within a parish community, however, the pilgrimage happens within our hearts.

Faith

Scripture On the Virtue
From the Holy Gospel according to John (20:29-31)

"Jesus said to him, "Have you come to believe because you have seen me? Blessed are those who have not seen and have believed." Now Jesus did many other signs in the presence of [his] disciples that are not written in this book. But these are written that you may [come to] believe that Jesus is the Messiah, the Son of God, and that through this belief you may have life in his name."

A Prayer for Faith
A Petition to Grow in Virtue

Lord, thank You for the gift of faith. I renew my confidence in Your goodness and plan for my life. Today I decide again to follow You, not knowing where You may lead, but with faith that You are always with me. Amen.

Personal Reflections
Take a few moments to speak to God about your life.

1. I quiet my heart and listen to the Word of God. Where is God speaking to me through this passage?

2. I thank God for His gifts. How is He already helping me to live this virtue? Can I think of a concrete way to improve?

3. Jesus, where do You want to strengthen my faith? When do I live as if God didn't exist? I renew my faith in the salvation You offer me out of love. Help me to live with my eyes focused on pleasing You.

Today's Journal
Spiritual Insights, Prayer Requests, Gratitude, Resolutions

_____

_____

_____

_____

_____

_____

_____

_____

_____

_____

_____

_____

_____

_____

_____

_____

_____

_____

_____

_____

_____

_____

_____

Humility

Scripture On the Virtue
From a Letter of St. Paul to the Philippians (2:3-5)

"Do nothing out of selfishness or out of vainglory; rather, humbly regard others as more important than yourselves, each looking out not for his own interests, but [also] everyone for those of others. Have among yourselves the same attitude that is also yours in Christ Jesus."

A Prayer for Humility
A Petition to Grow in Virtue

Jesus, help me to see myself as You do. Give me gratitude for the things that are good in me because they are Your gifts and come from Your generosity. Grant me a humble heart that makes me a gift to others. Amen.

Personal Reflections
Take a few moments to speak to God about your life.

1. I quiet my heart and listen to the Word of God. Where is God speaking to me through this passage?

2. I thank God for His gifts. How is He already helping me to live this virtue? Can I think of a concrete way to improve?

3. Lord, do I see myself only as You see me? Where has pride taken hold of my heart? I want to learn to accept Your blessings with humility. Teach me to serve others as You did.

Today's Journal
Spiritual Insights, Prayer Requests, Gratitude, Resolutions

Religion

Scripture On the Virtue
From the Holy Gospel according to Matthew (5:20-22)

"I tell you, unless your righteousness surpasses that of the scribes and Pharisees, you will not enter into the kingdom of heaven. You have heard that it was said to your ancestors, 'You shall not kill; and whoever kills will be liable to judgment.' But I say to you, whoever is angry with his brother will be liable to judgment, and whoever says to his brother, 'Raqa,' will be answerable to the Sanhedrin, and whoever says, 'You fool,' will be liable to fiery Gehenna."

A Prayer for Religion
A Petition to Grow in Virtue

Lord Jesus, teach me to have reverence and awe for Your holy name and Your sacred mysteries. Help me to approach You with humility and adoration. Help me to honor You in all my thoughts, words, and actions. Amen.

Personal Reflections
Take a few moments to speak to God about your life.

1. I quiet my heart and listen to the Word of God. Where is God speaking to me through this passage?

2. I thank God for His gifts. How is He already helping me to live this virtue? Can I think of a concrete way to improve?

3. Jesus, do I treat you as a close friend in everything that I do? Where do I lack reverence for God and His holy things? I renew my love for You and all Your gifts, Lord! Give me the grace to never be ashamed of belonging to You.

Today's Journal
Spiritual Insights, Prayer Requests, Gratitude, Resolutions

_____

_____

_____

_____

_____

_____

_____

_____

_____

_____

_____

_____

_____

_____

_____

_____

_____

_____

_____

_____

Interior Silence

Scripture On the Virtue
From the Book of Psalms (25:1-5)

"To you, O LORD, I lift up my soul, my God, in you I trust; do not let me be disgraced; do not let my enemies gloat over me. No one is disgraced who waits for you, but only those who lightly break faith. Make known to me your ways, LORD; teach me your paths. Guide me by your fidelity and teach me, for you are God my savior, for you I wait all the day long."

A Prayer for Interior Silence
A Petition to Grow in Virtue

God, grant me the gift of interior silence, that I may always listen to Your voice and discern Your will for my life. Help me to avoid idle gossip and to use my words to build up and encourage others. Amen.

Personal Reflections
Take a few moments to speak to God about your life.

1. I quiet my heart and listen to the Word of God. Where is God speaking to me through this passage?

2. I thank God for His gifts. How is He already helping me to live this virtue? Can I think of a concrete way to improve?

3. Jesus, I reflect on your example of silence during the early years of your life. Do I value the virtue of interior silence and reflection? Where do I allow noise to distract me from what matters most? I renew my desire to be led by You, Lord! Give me a humble and discerning heart.

Today's Journal
Spiritual Insights, Prayer Requests, Gratitude, Resolutions

_____

_____

_____

_____

_____

_____

_____

_____

_____

_____

_____

_____

_____

_____

_____

_____

_____

_____

_____

_____

_____

_____

Simplicity

Scripture On the Virtue
From the Holy Gospel according to Matthew (18:1-5)

"At that time the disciples approached Jesus and said, 'Who is the greatest in the kingdom of heaven?' He called a child over, placed it in their midst, and said, 'Amen, I say to you, unless you turn and become like children, you will not enter the kingdom of heaven. Whoever humbles himself like this child is the greatest in the kingdom of heaven. And whoever receives one child such as this in my name receives me.'"

A Prayer for Simplicity
A Petition to Grow in Virtue

Holy Spirit, help me to live a life of simplicity and detachment from the things of this world. Teach me to seek first the kingdom of God and to trust in the Father's providence for all my needs. Amen.

Personal Reflections
Take a few moments to speak to God about your life.

1. I quiet my heart and listen to the Word of God. Where is God speaking to me through this passage?

2. I thank God for His gifts. How is He already helping me to live this virtue? Can I think of a concrete way to improve?

3. Holy Spirit, do I see all things from Your wise and simple perspective? Where do I allow myself to worry about silly or unimportant things? I resolve to focus on what will lead me to heaven. Give me Your constant guidance in my everyday decisions.

Today's Journal
Spiritual Insights, Prayer Requests, Gratitude, Resolutions

_____

_____

_____

_____

_____

_____

_____

_____

_____

_____

_____

_____

_____

_____

_____

_____

_____

_____

_____

_____

_____

_____

Gratitude

Scripture On the Virtue
From a Letter of St. Paul to the Colossians (3:16-17)

"Let the word of Christ dwell in you richly, as in all wisdom you teach and admonish one another, singing psalms, hymns, and spiritual songs with gratitude in your hearts to God. And whatever you do, in word or in deed, do everything in the name of the Lord Jesus, giving thanks to God the Father through him."

A Prayer for Gratitude
A Petition to Grow in Virtue

Lord Jesus, help me to be grateful for all the blessings you have bestowed upon me, and to recognize that every good thing comes from you. Teach me to be generous with the gifts you have given me and to use them for the service of others. Amen.

Personal Reflections
Take a few moments to speak to God about your life.

1. I quiet my heart and listen to the Word of God. Where is God speaking to me through this passage?

2. I thank God for His gifts. How is He already helping me to live this virtue? Can I think of a concrete way to improve?

3. Jesus, do I find Your love for me in all the beautiful things I experience every day? What are the things that I enjoy the most that could help me find God through practicing gratitude? Lord, I want to see you in the things I enjoy. Give me gratitude that always leads me back to You.

Today's Journal
Spiritual Insights, Prayer Requests, Gratitude, Resolutions

Summary

Inspiration from these Virtues

What spiritual insights would I like to remember?

Resolutions from these Virtues

What practical ways did I find to help me grow?

Fiat

Our Response

Just like the Blessed Virgin Mary, our own lives require a response, a "fiat" to God's invitation. This requires trust and obedience.

The Meaning of this Glyph

Our response to God's invitation challenges us to embark upon a journey of faith. The path leads our hearts toward seeking and finding the purpose God has created us for.

Hope

Scripture On the Virtue
From the Book of Proverbs (3:5-8)

"Trust in the Lord with all your heart, on your own intelligence do not rely; In all your ways be mindful of him, and he will make straight your paths. Do not be wise in your own eyes, fear the Lord and turn away from evil; This will mean health for your flesh and vigor for your bones."

A Prayer for Hope
A Petition to Grow in Virtue

Father, You created me for heaven, but the storms of this life can make me lose my way. Help me trust that You are with me and strengthen my weaknesses with Your mercy and love. Give me confidence, remaining close to You. Amen.

Personal Reflections
Take a few moments to speak to God about your life.

1. I quiet my heart and listen to the Word of God. Where is God speaking to me through this passage?

2. I thank God for His gifts. How is He already helping me to live this virtue? Can I think of a concrete way to improve?

3. Father, where are You inviting me to have more trust in You? Are there any areas of my life where I rely more on other things or people to make me happy? I accept Your fatherly embrace and choose to respond to Your love. Give me the trust to always turn to You in my needs.

Today's Journal
Spiritual Insights, Prayer Requests, Gratitude, Resolutions

Obedience

Scripture On the Virtue
From the Letter of St. Paul to the Philippians (2:8-11)

"He humbled himself, becoming obedient to death, even death on a cross. Because of this, God greatly exalted him and bestowed on him the name that is above every name, that at the name of Jesus every knee should bend, of those in heaven and on earth and under the earth, and every tongue confess that Jesus Christ is Lord, to the glory of God the Father."

A Prayer for Obedience
A Petition to Grow in Virtue

Heavenly Father, help me to be obedient to Your will, like Your son Jesus, and to submit my own desires and plans to Your divine wisdom. Help me to trust in Your goodness and providence and to be faithful to your commandments. Amen.

Personal Reflections
Take a few moments to speak to God about your life.

1. I quiet my heart and listen to the Word of God. Where is God speaking to me through this passage?

2. I thank God for His gifts. How is He already helping me to live this virtue? Can I think of a concrete way to improve?

3. Father, do I always trust that Your will is the very best for me? Where do I go my own way? I choose to follow Your path for my life as given to me in the Bible and through the Church. Give me true wisdom, which helps me to rely on You in everything.

Today's Journal
Spiritual Insights, Prayer Requests, Gratitude, Resolutions

Meekness

Scripture On the Virtue
From the Letter of St. Paul to the Colossians (3:12-14)

"Put on then, as God's chosen ones, holy and beloved, compassionate hearts, kindness, humility, meekness, and patience, bearing with one another and, if one has a complaint against another, forgiving each other; as the Lord has forgiven you, so you also must forgive. And above all these put on love, which binds everything together in perfect harmony."

A Prayer for Meekness
A Petition to Grow in Virtue

Lord Jesus, teach me to be meek and gentle like You, who humbled Yourself and became a servant for our sake. Help me to bear with the weaknesses and faults of others and to respond to them with kindness and compassion. Amen.

Personal Reflections
Take a few moments to speak to God about your life.

1. I quiet my heart and listen to the Word of God. Where is God speaking to me through this passage?

2. I thank God for His gifts. How is He already helping me to live this virtue? Can I think of a concrete way to improve?

3. Lord, do I fear humility and meekness? Where do I prefer pride, selfishness, and vanity? I know it's hard, but I choose to imitate Your example of meekness. Help me to remember that You are always with me, giving me strength.

Today's Journal
Spiritual Insights, Prayer Requests, Gratitude, Resolutions

_____

_____

_____

_____

_____

_____

_____

_____

_____

_____

_____

_____

_____

_____

_____

_____

_____

_____

_____

_____

_____

_____

Generosity

Scripture On the Virtue
From the Letter of St. Paul to the Galatians (6:9-10)

"Let us not grow tired of doing good, for in due time we shall reap our harvest, if we do not give up. So then, while we have the opportunity, let us do good to all, but especially to those who belong to the family of the faith."

A Prayer for Generosity
A Petition to Grow in Virtue

Lord, thank You for being so generous with me. Today I renew my commitment to follow Your example. Help me to recognize opportunities to share and give from a selfless heart. Guide me to use my gifts wisely and with courage. Amen.

Personal Reflections
Take a few moments to speak to God about your life.

1. I quiet my heart and listen to the Word of God. Where is God speaking to me through this passage?

2. I thank God for His gifts. How is He already helping me to live this virtue? Can I think of a concrete way to improve?

3. Jesus, where can I better imitate Your example of generosity? Are there areas in my life where I am selfish with my things, my talents, or my time? I know that generosity will bring me true fulfillment and happiness. Teach me to think of others before myself.

Today's Journal
Spiritual Insights, Prayer Requests, Gratitude, Resolutions

_____

_____

_____

_____

_____

_____

_____

_____

_____

_____

_____

_____

_____

_____

_____

_____

_____

_____

_____

_____

_____

_____

_____

_____

Patience

Scripture On the Virtue
From the First Letter of St. Paul to the Corinthians (13:4-7)

"Love is patient, love is kind. It is not jealous, [love] is not pompous, it is not inflated, it is not rude, it does not seek its own interests, it is not quick-tempered, it does not brood over injury, it does not rejoice over wrongdoing but rejoices with the truth. It bears all things, believes all things, hopes all things, endures all things."

A Prayer for Patience
A Petition to Grow in Virtue

Jesus, give me patience when things don't go my way. Teach me to offer my sufferings as a sacrifice, united to Your sacrifice on the cross. Let me find peace in the situations I cannot control or change, because I trust in You. Amen.

Personal Reflections
Take a few moments to speak to God about your life.

1. I quiet my heart and listen to the Word of God. Where is God speaking to me through this passage?

2. I thank God for His gifts. How is He already helping me to live this virtue? Can I think of a concrete way to improve?

3. Lord, are there ways You are calling me to grow in patience? Where am I unkind towards others? Where do I only see short-term gains? Where does my life need more purpose? I resolve to patiently wait for Your timing in all things. Give me Your patience and peace.

Today's Journal
Spiritual Insights, Prayer Requests, Gratitude, Resolutions

_____

_____

_____

_____

_____

_____

_____

_____

_____

_____

_____

_____

_____

_____

_____

_____

_____

_____

_____

_____

_____

_____

_____

Prudence

Scripture On the Virtue
From the Book of Proverbs (14:16-19)

"The wise person is cautious and turns from evil, but the fool is reckless and arrogant. Quick-tempered people make fools of themselves, and schemers are hated. The simpleton inherits folly, but the prudent are crowned with knowledge. The evil bow down before the good, and the wicked at the gates of the just."

A Prayer for Prudence
A Petition to Grow in Virtue

Holy Spirit, teach me to listen to Your voice. Help me to wisely make decisions by seeking what You want instead of my own selfishness. Direct my actions so I look for happiness in what is truly good and right. Amen.

Personal Reflections
Take a few moments to speak to God about your life.

1. I quiet my heart and listen to the Word of God. Where is God speaking to me through this passage?

2. I thank God for His gifts. How is He already helping me to live this virtue? Can I think of a concrete way to improve?

3. Holy Spirit, where are You actively trying to guide me? Are there times that I don't even look for God's help when making important decisions? Holy Spirit, I renew my trust in Your ongoing support. Help me to learn docility to Your voice in everything I do.

Today's Journal
Spiritual Insights, Prayer Requests, Gratitude, Resolutions

Summary

Inspiration from these Virtues

What spiritual insights would I like to remember?

_____

_____

_____

_____

_____

_____

_____

_____

_____

_____

_____

_____

_____

_____

_____

_____

_____

_____

Resolutions from these Virtues

What practical ways did I find to help me grow?

Sacrifice

A Life of Self-Giving

As we give ourselves to God and our brothers and sisters in Christ as a means of sacrifice, we take on the responsibilities of justice. This response leads to true love and fortitude.

The Meaning of this Glyph

The path now becomes a hand. We realize that our journey requires genuine sacrifice of us and we respond by offering up our daily lives to God.

Love

Scripture On the Virtue
From the First Letter of St. Paul to the Corinthians (13:1-3)

"If I speak in human and angelic tongues but do not have love, I am a resounding gong or a clashing cymbal. And if I have the gift of prophecy and comprehend all mysteries and all knowledge, if I have all faith so as to move mountains but do not have love, I am nothing. If I give away everything I own, and if I hand my body over so that I may boast but do not have love, I gain nothing."

A Prayer for Love
A Petition to Grow in Virtue

Good Jesus, despite my sins, You want to be my friend. You give to everyone without ever judging or counting the cost. Give me a heart like Yours, willing to sacrifice myself for others as You did for me. Amen.

Personal Reflections
Take a few moments to speak to God about your life.

1. I quiet my heart and listen to the Word of God. Where is God speaking to me through this passage?

2. I thank God for His gifts. How is He already helping me to live this virtue? Can I think of a concrete way to improve?

3. Lord, do I really value Your infinite love for me? How do I show God that I love Him in my everyday life? I renew my gratitude for everything You have done for me, Jesus. Help me to respond to Your love by serving those around me with generosity.

Today's Journal
Spiritual Insights, Prayer Requests, Gratitude, Resolutions

Fortitude

Scripture On the Virtue
From the Book of Deuteronomy (31:6-7)

"Be strong and steadfast; have no fear or dread of them, for it is the LORD, your God, who marches with you; he will never fail you or forsake you. Then Moses summoned Joshua and in the presence of all Israel said to him, 'Be brave and steadfast, for you must bring this people into the land which the LORD swore to their ancestors he would give them; you must put them in possession of their heritage.'"

A Prayer for Fortitude
A Petition to Grow in Virtue

Dear Jesus, grant me wisdom to choose what is right; fortitude to persevere in goodness; and courage to patiently endure hardships. Help me to rely on Your guidance and strength with humility, as I imitate Your example of doing Your Father's will. Amen!

Personal Reflections
Take a few moments to speak to God about your life.

1. I quiet my heart and listen to the Word of God. Where is God speaking to me through this passage?

2. I thank God for His gifts. How is He already helping me to live this virtue? Can I think of a concrete way to improve?

3. With You, Oh Lord, I am always strong! When do I not allow You to accompany me? Are there moments when I try to go it alone? God, thank You for Your steadfast love for me. Help me to remain always close to You.

Today's Journal
Spiritual Insights, Prayer Requests, Gratitude, Resolutions

Temperance

Scripture On the Virtue
From the First Letter of St. Paul to the Corinthians (9:24-27)

"Do you not know that the runners in the stadium all run in the race, but only one wins the prize? Run so as to win. Every athlete exercises discipline in every way. They do it to win a perishable crown, but we an imperishable one. Thus I do not run aimlessly; I do not fight as if I were shadowboxing. No, I drive my body and train it, for fear that, after having preached to others, I myself should be disqualified."

A Prayer for Temperance
A Petition to Grow in Virtue

Jesus, as a man, You showed us that creation is good. Help me to imitate Your example of balance and moderation. Help me to enjoy the beauty and goodness of this world only as a path that leads me to You. Amen.

Personal Reflections
Take a few moments to speak to God about your life.

1. I quiet my heart and listen to the Word of God. Where is God speaking to me through this passage?

2. I thank God for His gifts. How is He already helping me to live this virtue? Can I think of a concrete way to improve?

3. Lord, am I running so as to win? Where do I treat this life as if I will automatically receive a prize? I recognize the spiritual battle between the flesh and the spirit. Give me, Lord, the strength to persevere!

Today's Journal
Spiritual Insights, Prayer Requests, Gratitude, Resolutions

_____

_____

_____

_____

_____

_____

_____

_____

_____

_____

_____

_____

_____

_____

_____

_____

_____

_____

_____

_____

_____

_____

Justice

Scripture On the Virtue
From the Book of the Prophet Isaiah (1:17-19)

"Learn to do good. Make justice your aim: redress the wronged, hear the orphan's plea, defend the widow. Come now, let us set things right, says the LORD: Though your sins be like scarlet, they may become white as snow; Though they be crimson red, they may become white as wool. If you are willing, and obey, you shall eat the good things of the land."

A Prayer for Justice
A Petition to Grow in Virtue

God, You give us the responsibility to care for the people around us. Help me to serve and care for their genuine good. Help me always keep Your words in my heart, "What you did to the least of these, you did for me." Amen.

Personal Reflections
Take a few moments to speak to God about your life.

1. I quiet my heart and listen to the Word of God. Where is God speaking to me through this passage?

2. I thank God for His gifts. How is He already helping me to live this virtue? Can I think of a concrete way to improve?

3. God, where do You ask me to be responsible for others in my life? Am I ever too busy to assist others or to take the time to stop and listen? I know that all mankind are my brothers and sisters in the Lord. Grant me the grace to genuinely care about those around me.

Today's Journal
Spiritual Insights, Prayer Requests, Gratitude, Resolutions

_____

_____

_____

_____

_____

_____

_____

_____

_____

_____

_____

_____

_____

_____

_____

_____

_____

_____

_____

_____

_____

_____

Chastity

Scripture On the Virtue
From the First Letter of St. Paul to the Corinthians (6:17-20)

"Whoever is joined to the Lord becomes one spirit with him. Avoid immorality. Every other sin a person commits is outside the body, but the immoral person sins against his own body. Do you not know that your body is a temple of the Holy Spirit within you, whom you have from God, and that you are not your own? For you have been purchased at a price. Therefore, glorify God in your body."

A Prayer for Chastity
A Petition to Grow in Virtue

Lord God, purify my heart and mind, that I may love what is good and true, and avoid all that is sinful and selfish. Help me to respect the dignity of every person, to see the beauty and goodness of your creation, and to live a life of purity in thought, word, and deed. Amen.

Personal Reflections
Take a few moments to speak to God about your life.

1. I quiet my heart and listen to the Word of God. Where is God speaking to me through this passage?

2. I thank God for His gifts. How is He already helping me to live this virtue? Can I think of a concrete way to improve?

3. Lord Jesus, thank You for coming to live within me through the gift of Baptism. Are there times that I forget that I am a temple of the Holy Spirit? Do I ever use my body only for pleasure? I remember that my body is God's gift. Give me the strength, Lord, to remain only Yours!

Today's Journal
Spiritual Insights, Prayer Requests, Gratitude, Resolutions

_____

_____

_____

_____

_____

_____

_____

_____

_____

_____

_____

_____

_____

_____

_____

_____

_____

_____

_____

_____

_____

_____

_____

Diligence

Scripture On the Virtue
From the Letter of St. Paul to the Colossians (3:23-25)

"Whatever you do, do from the heart, as for the Lord and not for others, knowing that you will receive from the Lord the due payment of the inheritance; be slaves of the Lord Christ. For the wrongdoer will receive recompense for the wrong he committed, and there is no partiality."

A Prayer for Diligence
A Petition to Grow in Virtue

Holy Spirit, inspire me with a spirit of diligence and hard work, that I may use my talents and gifts for the service of others. Help me to be responsible and patient, as I work to achieve the rewards that will last for eternity. Amen.

Personal Reflections
Take a few moments to speak to God about your life.

1. I quiet my heart and listen to the Word of God. Where is God speaking to me through this passage?

2. I thank God for His gifts. How is He already helping me to live this virtue? Can I think of a concrete way to improve?

3. Holy Spirit, am I willing to put in the hard work necessary to attain eternal life? Do I ever forget about eternity and get caught up in the pursuit of things that really don't matter? I want to make sure that I am willing to do my part, always relying on Your strength. Help me to give my very best.

Today's Journal
Spiritual Insights, Prayer Requests, Gratitude, Resolutions

Summary

Inspiration from these Virtues

What spiritual insights would I like to remember?

_____

_____

_____

_____

_____

_____

_____

_____

_____

_____

_____

_____

_____

_____

_____

_____

_____

_____

Resolutions from these Virtues

What practical ways did I find to help me grow?

_____

_____

_____

_____

_____

_____

_____

_____

_____

_____

_____

_____

_____

_____

_____

_____

_____

_____

_____

Transfiguration

Transformed into Christ
Like the examples we find in the saints, we too are called to be transformed into Christ, and to persevere in His name.

The Meaning of this Glyph
The sun reveals a cross, which transforms it into the Communion Host, and another hand appears. The sun and the hand represent how God's presence and action have entered our lives in concrete ways.

Charity

Scripture On the Virtue
From the First Letter of St. John (4:7-11)

"Beloved, let us love one another, because love is of God; everyone who loves is begotten by God and knows God. Whoever is without love does not know God, for God is love. In this way the love of God was revealed to us: God sent his only Son into the world so that we might have life through him. In this is love: not that we have loved God, but that he loved us and sent his Son as expiation for our sins. Beloved, if God so loved us, we also must love one another."

A Prayer for Charity
A Petition to Grow in Virtue

Heavenly Father, fill me with a desire to work for Your glory and the salvation of souls, that I may be a faithful witness to Your love and truth. Help me to share the Gospel with others, and to live a life of humble prayer and service. Amen.

Personal Reflections
Take a few moments to speak to God about your life.

1. I quiet my heart and listen to the Word of God. Where is God speaking to me through this passage?

2. I thank God for His gifts. How is He already helping me to live this virtue? Can I think of a concrete way to improve?

3. Jesus, am I grateful for my Catholic faith? Do I treasure Your gifts so much that I habitually share them with my family and friends? I know that true charity is about helping others to know and love God. Give me the strength to share Your love with the world.

Today's Journal
Spiritual Insights, Prayer Requests, Gratitude, Resolutions

Truthfulness

Scripture On the Virtue
From the Letter of St. Paul to the Ephesians (4:25,29-31)

"Therefore, putting away falsehood, speak the truth, each one to his neighbor, for we are members one of another. Let no evil talk come out of your mouths, but only what is useful for building up, as there is need, so that your words may give grace to those who hear. And do not grieve the Holy Spirit of God, with which you were marked with a seal for the day of redemption. Put away from you all bitterness and wrath and anger and wrangling and slander, together with all malice."

A Prayer for Truthfulness
A Petition to Grow in Virtue

Lord, grant me the integrity to always speak the truth in my words and to practice externally what I believe in my heart. May I always seek honesty and authenticity in my relationships. Guide me to embrace truth as a path to deeper communion with You and others. Amen.

Personal Reflections
Take a few moments to speak to God about your life.

1. I quiet my heart and listen to the Word of God. Where is God speaking to me through this passage?

2. I thank God for His gifts. How is He already helping me to live this virtue? Can I think of a concrete way to improve?

3. Jesus, am I always truthful in my words and actions? Are there moments when I'm afraid to stand up for what is right? I want to practice what I preach. Give me a greater love for truth and integrity.

Today's Journal
Spiritual Insights, Prayer Requests, Gratitude, Resolutions

_____

_____

_____

_____

_____

_____

_____

_____

_____

_____

_____

_____

_____

_____

_____

_____

_____

_____

_____

_____

_____

_____

_____

Kindness

Scripture On the Virtue
From the Letter of St. Paul to the Colossians (3:12-14)

"Put on then, as God's chosen ones, holy and beloved, heartfelt compassion, kindness, humility, gentleness, and patience, bearing with one another and forgiving one another, if one has a grievance against another; as the Lord has forgiven you, so must you also do. And over all these put on love, that is, the bond of perfection."

A Prayer for Kindness
A Petition to Grow in Virtue

Loving God, inspire us to embody kindness as a reflection of Your boundless love. Grant us the grace to grow in compassion and mercy towards others. Guide us on our journey of spreading kindness, that we may bring Your comfort to those in need. Amen.

Personal Reflections
Take a few moments to speak to God about your life.

1. I quiet my heart and listen to the Word of God. Where is God speaking to me through this passage?

2. I thank God for His gifts. How is He already helping me to live this virtue? Can I think of a concrete way to improve?

3. Holy Spirit, in what areas of my life do You desire to fill me with Your gifts? Am I sometimes selfish and greedy in the way I treat others? I want to imitate Jesus' way of service and kindness towards all mankind. Strengthen me with Your gifts; fill me that I might be more like Christ.

Today's Journal
Spiritual Insights, Prayer Requests, Gratitude, Resolutions

Forgiveness

Scripture On the Virtue

From the Holy Gospel according to Matthew (5:44-45, 6:14)

"But I say to you, love your enemies, and pray for those who persecute you, that you may be children of your heavenly Father, for he makes his sun rise on the bad and the good, and causes rain to fall on the just and the unjust. For if you forgive others their trespasses, your heavenly Father will forgive you."

A Prayer for Forgiveness

A Petition to Grow in Virtue

Divine Mercy, I humbly ask for your assistance in forgiving those who have wronged me, and in seeking forgiveness from those whom I have wronged. Please fill my heart with compassion for those who are suffering, and guide me to give them the same mercy and love that come from You. Amen.

Personal Reflections

Take a few moments to speak to God about your life.

1. I quiet my heart and listen to the Word of God. Where is God speaking to me through this passage?

2. I thank God for His gifts. How is He already helping me to live this virtue? Can I think of a concrete way to improve?

3. Merciful Jesus, am I grateful for Your sacrifice on the cross? When I am angry with others, do I sometimes forget about the forgiveness that You have shown me? I renew my desire to always be willing to forgive others. Lord, make my heart more like Yours!

Today's Journal
Spiritual Insights, Prayer Requests, Gratitude, Resolutions

Constancy

Scripture On the Virtue
From the Gospel according to Matthew (7:24-27)

"Everyone who listens to these words of mine and acts on them will be like a wise man who built his house on rock. The rain fell, the floods came, and the winds blew and buffeted the house. But it did not collapse; it had been set solidly on rock. And everyone who listens to these words of mine but does not act on them will be like a fool who built his house on sand."

A Prayer for Constancy
A Petition to Grow in Virtue

Lord, You are faithful to all Your promises. Please give me the gift of steadfast faith so that I may be constant in my commitment to You, even amid challenges. May I find comfort and strength in Your unwavering love and mercy. Amen.

Personal Reflections
Take a few moments to speak to God about your life.

1. I quiet my heart and listen to the Word of God. Where is God speaking to me through this passage?

2. I thank God for His gifts. How is He already helping me to live this virtue? Can I think of a concrete way to improve?

3. Jesus, am I fully committed to taking up my cross and following You? Do I ever look for ways to avoid my regular responsibilities? I commit anew to carry the crosses that God has allowed me to be responsible for. Lord, help me to always rely on your assistance.

Today's Journal

Spiritual Insights, Prayer Requests, Gratitude, Resolutions

Perseverance

Scripture On the Virtue
From the Letter of St. Paul to the Hebrews (12:1-2)

"Therefore, since we are surrounded by so great a cloud of witnesses, let us rid ourselves of every burden and sin that clings to us and persevere in running the race that lies before us while keeping our eyes fixed on Jesus, the leader and perfecter of faith. For the sake of the joy that lay before him he endured the cross, despising its shame, and has taken his seat at the right of the throne of God."

A Prayer for Perseverance
A Petition to Grow in Virtue

Lord God, grant me the strength to persevere in doing good, even in the face of obstacles, so that I can remain faithful to You and to Your commandments. Help me to trust in Your wisdom and guidance in all my responsibilities. Amen.

Personal Reflections
Take a few moments to speak to God about your life.

1. I quiet my heart and listen to the Word of God. Where is God speaking to me through this passage?

2. I thank God for His gifts. How is He already helping me to live this virtue? Can I think of a concrete way to improve?

3. God, being faithful is not easy. Am I aware that You are always faithful to me? Where am I weak and inconsistent in prayer, service, or gratitude? I commit again to belong to You in everything. Help me to persevere in the race, so that I can be with You one day in heaven.

Today's Journal
Spiritual Insights, Prayer Requests, Gratitude, Resolutions

Summary

Inspiration from these Virtues

What spiritual insights would I like to remember?

Resolutions from these Virtues

What practical ways did I find to help me grow?

134